Gardeners' G
Growing Peas

A Guide Book for Planting, Growing and Harvesting Peas

Gardener's Guide to Growing Your Vegetable Garden – Book XII

Paul R. Wonning

Gardeners' Guide to Growing Peas

Published By Paul R. Wonning
Copyright 2017 by Paul R. Wonning
Print Edition

mossyfeetbooks@gmail.com

If you would like email notification of when new Mossy Feet books become available email the author for inclusion in the subscription list.

Mossy Feet Books
www.mossyfeetbooks.com

Indiana Places

http://indianaplaces.blogspot.com/

Description

The *Gardeners' Guide to Growing Peas* has all the information the gardener needs to grow, harvest and preserve the pea in the vegetable garden. Like the other vegetable planting guides, Gardeners' *Guide to Growing Peas* is an excellent book for veteran and beginning gardeners to learn the culture of growing peas.

Table of Contents

Also in this Series
Gardener's Guide to Growing Your Vegetable Garden
Gardeners' Guide to Growing the Tomato
Gardeners Guide to Growing Green Beans
Gardener's Guide to Growing Potatoes in the Vegetable Garden
Gardeners Guide to Growing Cabbage in the Vegetable Garden
Gardeners Guide to Growing to the Carrot
Gardener's Guide to the Cucumber
Gardener's Guide to Growing Sweet Potatoes
Gardener's Guide to Growing Onions in the Vegetable Garden
Gardeners' Guide Book Growing and Harvesting Lettuce
Gardener's Guide to Growing Zuchini and Summer Squash
Gardeners' Guide to Growing Peas
Gardener's Guide to the Pepper
Gardener's Guide to the Pumpkin and Winter Squash
Gardeners' Guide to Growing Sweet Corn
Gardener's Guide to Growing Beets
Gardener's Guide to Growing Turnips
Gardener's Guide to the Cauliflower, Brocooli and other Cole Crops
Gardener's Guide to the Eggplant
Gardener's Guide to the Radish
Gardener's Guide to the Spinach and other Greens

Gardeners' Guide to the Pea

Paul R. Wonning

Introduction

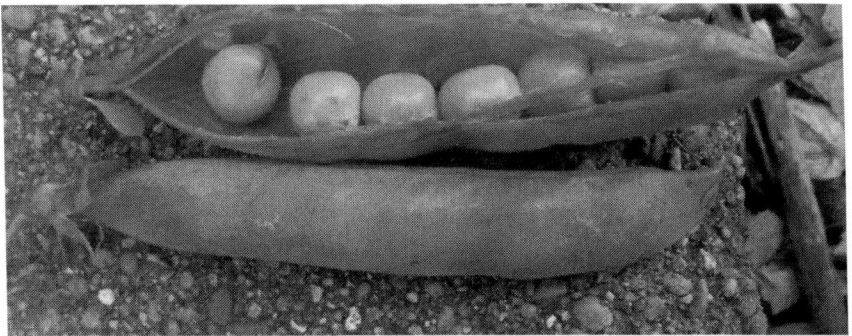

People have grown peas since ancient times, first as a staple, as dried pea for use in soups and stews, then later, with the development of the garden pea, as a fresh vegetable. The nitrogen fixing ability of the roots allows the pea to grow in less than desirable soils. This ability then improves the soil for other crops, as some of this nitrogen stays in the soil. Today, gardeners grow garden peas for used in salads, casseroles and other dishes. They are also good steamed or cooked as a standalone vegetable. Dried peas are useful in soups and stew, while the newer "snap peas" have sweet, edible pods as well as the tasty seeds inside. Best grown in cool weather, gardeners can grow them for an early crop, with other vegetables following them after harvest, or as a fall crop planted after other early crops have gone.

Common Name:

Pea

The word pea derives from the Latin work, pisum. This name in turn originates from the Greek word, pison. The English transformed this into their name, pease. Since this word is a plural form of the word, the English dropped the "s." Thus, they call the vegetable a "pea," the singular form of the word pease.

Botanical Name:

Pisum sativum

The botanical name stems from the Latin word for pea, pisum. The generic name, sativum, is the Latin word meaning "cultivated."

Family:

Leguminosae, Fabaceae

Fabaceae is a new name fixed by botanists that derives from the Latin word "bean." Leguminosae is an older name, still used, which is a Latin term that refers to the fruit.

The Fabaceae family is a large family that consists of annual, perennial plants, trees, vines and herbs. It is the third largest plant family with 630 genera and over 18,860 species. Many of the members of this family have great economic importance. These include peas, beans, soybeans, licorice, alfalfa and clover. Most members of this family have a fruit that botanists refer to as a legume. This seeds developed inside a pod that has two seams. Several seeds usually inhabit each pod. Most members of this family also host bacteria called rhizobia in nodules on their roots. These bacteria have the important function of taking nitrogen from the air and converting it to a form that most plants can use. This trait makes legumes an important part of a gardeners' plant rotation. These bacteria convert more nitrogen than their hosts can use. The remainder of the nitrogen stays in the soil after the plant has completed its life cycle, making it available to other plants.

Light:

Full sun

Soil:

Since peas fix their own nitrogen, it is not necessary for them to have especially fertile soil. They do benefit from a loose, well-drained soil.

Hardiness Zone:

Peas are an annual, so there USDA has not set a hardiness zone. The pea is quite cold tolerant. It will stand cold temperatures down to about 25 degrees Fahrenheit. If the plants have a covering of snow, they could survive temperatures as low as 10 degrees Fahrenheit.

Origins and History:

The pea originated in the Mediterranean and Near East area. Traditionally, peas were allowed to dry. People usually ate them as pease porridge, a pudding type dish, and in pea soup. Scientists have found the earliest archeological evidence of peas grown as food dates from about 4400 to 4800 BC. in the Nile region of Egypt. Archeologists have also found evidence of peas in the Georgian region of Russia. Fresh, green peas appeared sometime in the 1700's and were considered a luxury food and called "garden peas," as opposed to "field peas," grown to dry for soups.

Propagation:

Propagation of peas is by planting seeds.

Plant Height, Spread, Spacing:

Plant Height: Eighteen inches to ten feet or more, depending upon variety. Vining varieties need a trellis for support.

Spread: Six to eight inches

Spacing: Space the seeds about two to three inches apart, thin the seedlings to about four inches.

Flower Color, Description and Fragrance:

The flowers appear in clusters of two to six per cluster. Some varieties may have White, blue, pink, lavendar, violet or purple. The flowers have an equal number of seperate petals and sepals, usually five, sometimes four, again depending upon varieties. Modern peas have very little fragrance.

Plant Description:

The pea is a vining or trailing plant with alternate leaves borne on short stalks. Tendrils support the sprawling vines, holding the hollow stemmed plant off the ground if support is provided.

Pollination:

Peas have perfect flowers, meaning that each flower has male and female parts. Most peas will self-pollinate without the need of insect or other pollinators.

Nitrogen-fixing ability

Peas, and other legumes garden plants like beans, have the ability to take nitrogen in the atmosphere and fix it in the soil. The plants do this by using bacteria located in nodules on the plants roots. This symbiotic relationship is beneficial to both the legumes and the bacteria. The bacteria take nitrogen from the oxygen and, by a complex chemical process, convert it to ammonia. Ammonia is nitrogen in a form that plants can use it. The plants pay the bacteria back by supplying sugars to the bacteria that it needs to survive. The bacteria are a special kind called Rhizobium bacteria. The bacteria are specific to the plant, thus the Rhizobium bacteria that peas need are a different species from the ones that beans require. This bacteria is usually present in garden soil.

Deficiencies of *Rhizobium*

If the type of legume you are planting has not been planted in the garden before, if it is a new plot or you have not planted the plant before it is possible that these bacteria are not present. Using chemical fertilizers or pesticides can also kill the bacteria. To ensure that the bacterium is present, you may coat the seed with an innoculant that contains the correct bateria at seed planting time. The innoculant sold in garden stores and mail order seed supply companies usually contain a mix of bacteria that will inoculate most garden crops. These inoculants are inexpensive. The inoculants will have an expiration date and must be stored properly for them to survive. The species needed for most garden crops are:

Common Beans - *R. leguminosarum bv. phaseoli*

Field or Garden Peas - *R. leguminosarum bv viciae*

Peanut - *Bradyrhizobium sp.*

Chickpeas - *Mesorhizobium sp.*

Soybeans - *Bradyrhizobium japonicum*

To use, moisten the seed and dust the innoculant over it. mix it in well and plant immediately. You can also sprinkle the innoculant into the soil where you are planting the seeds. Work it in well. Some seeds are pre-inoculated, so check the seed packet, which will state it on the package if it is. Store unused innoculant in a sealed plastic bag in an area with consistent temperatures. A refrigerator will work. Properly stored, the innoculant should keep for a year.

Legume crops like peas and beans will fix more nitrogen in the soil than they need. This nitrogen is available for future crops grown in the garden and can reduce fertilizer for other vegetables. Farmers have taken advantage of this nitrogen fixing ability for generations by rotating legume crops with other field crops.

Planting Seeds:

Peas grow best in cool, sunny weather. The seed will germinate in cool soil, so plant the seeds as early as you can work the soil. If the garden tends to lie wet, as most do during the early spring, use raised beds or mounds to elevate the planting and preventing the seed from rotting. Work the soil in the fall, if possible. Work the soil to about four inches deep and apply a generous layer of compost. Plant the seed about one and a half inches deep. Poke a hole in the soil with a dibble or dowel, drop the seed in and close the hole. Plant the seeds about two inches apart.

Growing Seedlings:

The seedlings will need little care other than thinning to about six inches or so apart. Start training them to a trellis when they are about six inches tall. Peas do not transplant well, so no advantage is gained by starting in pots. Peas need to be planted early here in southeastern Indiana. Mid February is not too early if you can get into the garden. Peas are very hardy and are not bothered by cold, or even a light covering over newly germinated seedlings. To plant early, just poke a hole in the ground about an inch or so deep, and drop in a pea. Space them about two inches apart. The peas must be planted early because they do not like hot weather at all. Temperatures above seventy degrees will cause production to drop

Garden Culture and Uses:

After training, peas need little care, other than irrigation and watching for pests, until harvest. Try not to hoe close to the plants, as the roots are fragile and easily damaged. Trellising the plants before they start to vine will keep the plants off the ground. This will minimize cleaning the harvested pea pods, make harvest easier and cut down on disease.

Problems:

Peas have few problems in the garden, however there are a few insects and diseases which can afflict them. These include"

Fusarium wilt

Affected Area:

Leaf

Description:

The lower leaves will become stunted and turn yellow. The plant will usually die.

Control:

Pull up and destroy infected plants. Do not compost the plants. Rotate planting location. Use disease-resistant varieties.

Powdery Mildew

Affected Area:

Leaf

Description:

Leaves will develop a white, powdery growth on top.

Control:

Use sulfur dust on affected plants and destroy them. Do not compost. Use seed treated with fungicide.

Problem:

Aphanomyces Root Rot

Affected Area:

Root

Description:

Straw colored lesions will form on the roots, discoloring the entire root system over time.

Control: There are no resistant cultivars or cures for this disease. Try to avoid infected soil, if possible.

Problem:

Bean Leaf Roll Virus

Affected Area:

The entire above ground portion of the plant.

Description:

The plant will be stunted, often dying before they bloom. The plant will yellow, then collapse.

Control:

Use resistant cultivars.

Problem:

Downy Mildew

Affected

Area:

Leaf

Description:

Fungus begins to grow all over the plant, stunting and yellowing it. Eventually green, yellow or brown lesions form.

Control:

Use resistant cultivars. Fungicides are useful for severe infestation.

Problem:

Pea Seedborne Mosaic

Affected Area:

Entire Plant

Description:

The plants become stunted and malformed, dying before they bloom.

Control:

Use resistant cultivars.

Problem:

Pea Stunt

Affected Area: Entire Plant

Description: This disease kills young plants very early before they get a chance to bloom. As the plants become older, the infections will cause stunted growth and terminal rotting.

Control: The best method of control is to use resistant cultivars.

Problem:

Powdery Mildew

Affected Area:

Leaf

Description:

Small lesions develop on the plants on the lowest leaves. The lesions develop a white, powdery looking areas.

Control:

Use resistant varieties. Chemical controls include benomyl or sulfur, but must be properly timed to be effective. Plant early and use sprinkler irrigation. This should minimize the chances of having a crop infected with powdery mildew.

Problem:

Rhizoctonia Solani Seedling Rot

Affected Area:

Seed

Description:

Reddish brown to brown watery-looking lesions appear, girdling the plant. The plants will become stunted and usually die.

Control:

Use seed treated with fungicide or use pre-treated seed. Captan is recommended.

Aphids

An aphid infestation can quickly grow rapidly. These green, yellow, brown or reddish colored insects use their pointed mouths to suck plant juices, weakening and disfiguring the plant. They can also transmit many viral diseases like mosaic and pea leaf roll.

Controls:

Insecticidal soap, neem oil are useful. Ladybugs consume the insects. Releasing them from commercial growers may help, but many times the lady bugs simply fly off to other parts.

Pea weevils

Pea weevils emerge in the spring and lay their eggs in the pea seeds. The larvae will eat the seas, creating visible holes. There is no control. If afflicted, a row cover over freshly planted beds may keep the insects away from the seed.

The pea leaf weevil attacks both roots and leaves of the plant. Larvae feed on the nitrogen-providing nodules of the plant. Adults appear as a gray-brown bug with a trio of stripes down its back and the infected plant will have notches in foliage.

Leafminer

The gardener will notice trails and tunnels in the leaves. Leafminer larvae tunnel inside leaves. Destroy infected leaves and cultivate the garden to destroy larvae and keep adult flies from laying eggs. Cover crops with floating row covers

Medicinal uses:"

Weight Management:

Peas are low fat but high everything else. A cup of peas has less than 100 calories but has an abundance of protein, fiber and micronutrients.

Stomach cancer prevention:

Peas contain high amounts of a health-protective polyphenol called coumestrol. One study has determined you only need two milligrams per day of this nutrient to prevent stomach cancer. A cup of peas has at least 10.

Anti-aging, strong immune system, and high energy:

This comes from the high levels of anti-oxidants including:

Flavinoids

Carotenoid

Phenolic acids

Polyphenols

A diet rich in peas helps retard wrinkles, alzheimer's, arthritis, bronchitis, osteoporosis and candida.

Peas strong anti-inflammatory properties help with these problems.. Excess inflammation has also been linked to, heart disease, cancer, and aging in general. Peas have Pisumsaponins I II as well as pisomosides A and B. These substances are anti-inflammatory phytonutrients are found almost exclusively in peas.

Peas have both vitamin C and E, They also have generous amouts of the anti-oxidant mineral zinc omega-3 fat in the form of alpha-linolenic acid.

Blood sugar regulation:

High fibre slows and protein slows down how fast the body digests sugars.

The anti-oxidants and anti-inflammatory help prevent type 2 diabetes.

All carbohydrates are natural sugars and starches with no white sugars or chemicals.

Heart disease prevention:

The antioxidant and anti-inflammatory compounds support healthy blood vessels, helping reduce the formation of plaque along blood vessel walls.

Peas also contain vitamin B1 and folate, B2, B3, and B6. These vitamins help reduce homocysteine levels which are risk factor for heart disease.

Prevent constipation

The high fiber content in peas improves bowel health movement.

9. Healthy bones

One cup of peas contains 44% of the daily requirement of Vitamin K. This helps to anchor calcium inside the bones. This trait can also help reduce osteoporosis symptoms.

Reduce bad cholesterol:

The niacin in peas helps reduce, the production of triglycerides and low-density lipoprotein. This can result in in less bad cholesterol, increased cholesterol, and lower triglycerides.

Food Uses:

Garden peas have many food uses. Steam or boil them, make pea soup, or use raw in salads. Many cooks like to add them to cassaroles, pot pies and other dishes. The peas are delicious right from the garden, just shell them and pop them into your mouth. gardeners may allow them to dry on the vine and use in soups and stews.

Harvesting:

Gardeners will want to pick peas while the peas are young and tender. Press the side of the pod gently. When you can feel that the pod has filled out, pick them before the pod color begins to fade. When the peas are too mature, they tend to be tough and not as sweet. When the peas are ripening, daily harvest is necessary. Harvest snowpeas before the pods fill completely. For dried peas, allow the pods to remain on the vine until they turn brown and dry. Pick them and allow to dry before removing from the pods.

Shell them by holding the pea seam side out and pressing the seam with the thumb. the seam will split, opening the pod. Using your thumb, strip the peas from the pod into a bowl.

Storage:

Do not shell fresh peas that you intend to store. Wash the pods and place in a sealed container. Place in the refrigerator. They should keep a couple of days. The sugar in peas converts to starch quite quickly, so eat them as soon as possible.

Freezing Peas

There is nothing complicated about freezing peas. Choose fresh picked peas, rinse them and then shell them. You will need about seven pounds of peas, before shelling, to produce seven quarts of peas. Place a pot filled about two thirds full of water on the stove and bring it to a boil. While the water is heating up, prepare another bowl of ice water filled one-half to two thirds full. Pour the peas into the boiling water, blanching them. This destroys the bacteria and enzymes that would eventually ruin the peas. Boil the peas for about ninety seconds. Do not blanch too long, as this will overcook them and make them mushy. Remove the peas from the water by using a strainer or pouring through a colander. You may save the boiling water in a larger pot for reuse. Next, dump the peas in the ice water. This stops the cooking process immediately. Pour into freezer bags or container, label, date and place in the freezer. Frozen peas will keep for several months.

Canning Peas

To can peas you will need:

Pressure Canner

Canning Jars

Canning Seals And Rings

Jar Lifter

Canning Funnel

Large Pot

Bowls

Large Spoons

Sharp Knife

Towels And Dish Cloths

For one canner load of seven quarts of peas, you will need thirty-one pounds of fresh peas. This is approximately one bushel of peas. For nine pints, you will need twenty pounds of peas. Shell and wash the peas, as you would for freezing peas. Gardeners unfamiliar with canning vegetables, it is advisable to go to this link and read the information available there.

http://nchfp.uga.edu/publications/usda/GUIDE01_Home Can_rev0715.pdf

A pressure canner is recommended. It takes less time and produces results that are more consistent. To raw pack in a pressure canner, fill the jars with the fresh peas using the canning funnel and add boiling water to the jar. Leave one inch of space at the top. Do not shake the jars or press the peas down. Put the lid on the jars and screw down the rings. Wipe the rim of the jars down first with a clean cloth. Place the filled jars in the pressure canner and put on the lid. Read the instructions for your pressure canner before canning.

The altitude of your location will determine pressure needed to process the peas. If using a weighted pressure canner, process for forty minutes at ten pounds of pressure at 1000 feet above sea level. If you are above 1000 feet, process forty minutes at fifteen pounds pressure. For a dial gauge canner, process for forty minutes at eleven pounds for altitudes of 0 - 2000 feet, twelve pounds at 2000 to 4000 feet altitude, thirteen pounds at 4000 to 6000 feet and 14 pounds for 6000 feet and above.

When the time completes, turn off the heat and allow the canner to cool and depressurize naturally. When the canner depressurized, and this will take a while, remove the lids. Using the jar lifter, lift the jars out of the canner and place on a towel on a counter top. The jars will be quite hot, so be careful. As the jars cool, you should hear "popping" sounds as the jars seal. When cool, press the center of the lid. If it does not press down, the jar has sealed. If not, it did not seal. Place in the refrigerator and use within a few days. Alternatively, process any that did not seal for the full processing time again.

Canned peas should keep for a year or somewhat more stored in a cool, dark place.

Note: Read the manual that comes with your canner for full instructions and further precautions. This link at Pick Your Own has PDF downloads for many popular canners.

Drying Peas

It is possible to dry peas using a food dehydrator. Start with ripe, unblemished peas. Shell and steam them until the skins begin to form indentations. Place in a single layer on dehydrator trays. Set the temperature between 125 and 135 degrees, unless the instructions on your dehydrator say different. Dry until the peas are brittle, remembering to rotate the trays periodically to ensure consistent drying. It should take between five and fifteen hours to dry them. Store in a sealed container the dried peas should keep for several months in a cool, dark location.

Another method is to allow them to dry on the vine. When the pods are dry, shell and store in sealed container or bags in a cool, dark place.

Re-hydrate by pouring boiling water on them and soaking them for about half an hour, or until they have plumped up. Use in salads, as a cooked vegetable or in soups.

Groups:

Shelling Peas

Shelling peas are peas meant to be shelled and eaten fresh from the pod. The pods are not eaten.

Alderman Peas

Tall Telephone - 85 days

Tall Telephone will climb a six to eight foot trellis. The huge pods, each filled with six to eight peas, are easy to harvest and shell.

Serge Peas - 68 days

Top-of-the-line is a shelling pea for fresh eating and processing.

Maestro Peas - 60 days

Maestro allows multiple pickings, and it is easy to see which pods are ready since they tend to stick out on the vine.

Half Pint Peas - 50 days

Also known as Tom Thumb, this rare heirloom shelling pea is a dwarf pea. It will grow six to eight inches tall.

Green Arrow Peas - 70 days, 250 days fall sown.

Green Arrow Peas is an heirloom, disease resistant variety.

Canoe Peas - 70 days spring sown. 250 days fall sown.

Canoe packs a lot of peas per pound.

Lincoln Peas - 67 days

An English heirloom variety, also called Homesteader, is still a sweet shelling pea.

Edible-Podded Snow

Snap Peas

Southern Peas -- Black-Eyeds, Crowders And Cream

Early Frosty Pea (60 Days)

Carouby De Maussane Pea (65 Days) (Heirloom)

Green Arrow Pea (63 Days)

Knight Pea (56 Days)

Tom Thumb Pea (50-55 Days) (Heirloom

Edible-Podded Snow Peas

Also called Chinese Pod Peas, edible podded snow peas have edible pods in addition to the sweet tasting pea inside. Like string beans, Cooks usually remove the "string" that runs along the seam of the pod. Include thee flat podded peas in stir fry dishes and salads. Consume the mild flavored snow peas raw or cooked.

Golden Sweet 60-70 days

Oregon Sugar Pod II Peas - 70 days spring sown. 250 days fall sown. Easy to grow, non-climbing dwarf vines grow to approximately 30 inches tall.

Sweet Horizon Peas - 60-70 days

This gourmet quality snow pea was bred in European style It will develop beautiful laser-straight flat pods.

Little Snowpea White Pea - 30 days

This is an incredibly early variety.

Little Snowpea Purple Pea - 50-54 days

Semi-dwarf, this pea grows twenty-four inches tall.

Mammoth Melting Sugar Snow Pea (Heirloom, 65-75 Days)

Oregon Giant Snow Pea (65 Days)

Snap Peas

Also called sugar snap peas the pods of this pea, like snow peas, is edible. Developed as a cross between snow peas and shelling peas, these peas differ from snow peas in that the pods become rounded, like shelling peas instead of flat like snow peas. The pods do not have as much fiber as shelling peas, thus are tender and sweet when harvested young.

Pea-Ples Choice Mix

Sugar Ann Peas - 55 days spring sown. 235 days fall sown.

Sugar Ann Pea is a non-climbing, early and easy-to-grow snap pea.

Cascadia Peas - 60 days, 229 days fall sown.

Sugar Daddy Peas - 65 days

A genuinely stringless snap pea, with uniform, 24 inch plants.

Sugar Sprint Peas - 55 days

Super Sugar Snap Peas - 58 days

Sugar Bon Peas - 56 days

This early, dwarf snap pea is a strong yielder of very sweet and flavorful 3 inch pods.

Cascadia Snap Pea (48 Days)

Sugar Lace Ii Snap Pea (65 Days)

Super Sugar Snap Pea (62 Days)

Cow Pea - Black-eyed Pea

The cow pea and its related Black Eyed Pea, is an important food crop world wide. Cowpeas have been used as food since ancient times. The peas may be consumed raw, like shelling peas, or allowed to dry. The most common use is to allow them to dry on the vine, then shell out and store for use in soups and stews and various Asian dishes.

Colossus

Calif. Blackeye #5

Alabama Giant Blackeye

Calhoun P. Hull

Calico

Colossus

Pinkeye P. Hull

Mississippi Silver2

Texas Cream 82

Calif Blackeye

Nutrition:

Amount Per 1 cup (145 g)

Calories 118

% Daily Value*

Total Fat 0.6 g - 0%

Saturated fat 0.1 g - 0%

Polyunsaturated fat - 0.3 g

Monounsaturated fat - 0.1 g

Cholesterol 0 mg - 0%

Sodium 7 mg - 0%

Potassium 354 mg - 10%

Total Carbohydrate 21 g - 7%

Dietary fiber 7 g - 28%

Sugar - 8 g

Protein 8 g - 16%

Vitamin A - 22%

Vitamin C - 96%

Calcium - 3%

Iron - 11%

Vitamin D - 0%

Vitamin B-6 - 10%

Vitamin B-12 - 0%

Magnesium - 12%

*Percent Daily Values are based on a 2,000 calorie diet. Your daily values may be higher or lower depending on your calorie needs.

Seed Companies to Buy Pea Seed:

Burpee

W. Atlee Burpee Company

Warminster PA 18974

1-800-888-1447

The W. Atlee Burpee Company is one of the leading seed companies

in the gardening industry. The catalog lists good selections of annual and

perennial flowers as well as vegetable seeds. Many, many tomatoes listed in

addition to sweet corn and squash.

http://www.burpee.com/

Farmers Seed and Nursery

Division of Plantron, Inc

818 NW 4th Street

Fairbault, MN 55021

1-850-7334-1623

This catalog has a good selection of nursery stock including ornamental shrubs and trees. Fruit includes strawberries, blackberries and raspberries. Other types of fruit trees and vines, too. Nut trees, perennial plants and roses, also. There is a good selection of vegetable seed.

http://www.farmerseed.com/

George W. Park Seed Company

1 Parkton Ave

Greenwood, SC 29647-0001

1-800-845-3369

This bountiful catalog has extensive offerings of all categories of seeds - herbs, vegetables, annual and perennial seeds. There is also a generous offering of fruit and berry plants like grapes, blackberries and strawberries.

http://www.parkseed.com/

Gurney's Seed and Nursery

PO Box 4178

Greendale, IN 47025-4178

513-354-1491

Gurney's large format catalog offers large selections of vegetables, flowers, fruits and supplies for gardening. They also list trees, shrubs, roses, and nut trees. This is one of the older seed companies, they have been selling seeds for many years.

http://www.gurneys.com/

Harris Seeds

355 Paul Road

PO Box 24966

Rochester, NY 14624-0966

1-800-514-4441

Heavy selection of vegetable seeds, with a nice offering of flower seeds, too. They have almost 20 pages of gardening supplies like seed starting equipment, flats and carts.

http://www.harrisseeds.com/

John Scheepers Kitchen Garden Seeds

23 Tulip Drive

PO Box 838

Bantam, CT 06750-0638

1-860-567-6086

www.kitchengardenseeds.com

This catalog focuses on vegetables and herbs. It has unusual and old time varieties as well as some of the favorites. The salad green selection of seeds is excellent. There are also Asian greens and sprouting seeds. There are some flower seeds, mostly annual fragrant and cutting flowers. This is a nice catalog with some unusual seed offerings.

Johnny's Selected Seeds

955 Benton Ave.

Winslow, ME 04901

Phone: 877-564-6697

Fax: 800-738-6314

Annuals

Bulbs

Perennials

Flower, Vegetable and Wildflower Seeds

Fruit Trees and Berries

Garden Supplies, Tools and Power Equipment

Gifts and Decorative Accessories

Greenhouses and Indoor Gardening Supplies

Ground Covers, Shrubs, Trees, and Vines

Herbs and Vegetables

Irrigation Supplies and Equipment

Fertilizer, Weed & Pest Control Products

Magazines and Books

Ornamental Grasses and Plants

Johnny's Selected Seeds is a mail-order seed producer and merchant located in Albion and Winslow, Maine, USA. The company was established in 1973 by our Founder and Chairman Rob Johnston, Jr. Johnny's prides itself on its superior product, research, technical information, and service for home gardeners and commercial growers.

Our products include vegetable seeds, medicinal and culinary herb seeds, and flower seeds. We also offer unique, high quality gardening tools and supplies. Our Export Department ships seeds internationally, and welcomes your inquiry. Of course, we also ship throughout the United States. We sell both retail and wholesale, small to large quantities.

Website: Johnnyseeds.com

Email Contact: homegarden@johnnyseeds.com

J. W. Jung Seed Company

335 South High Street

Randolph, WI 53957-0001

1-800-247-5864

http://www.jungseed.com/

Jung sells a very interesting mix of fruit trees and plants, shrubs and trees, vegetable and flower seed, and gardening supplies. Perennial plants, flower bulbs, lilies and roses are included in the offerings. This is a "must have" catalog for the gardener.

Pinetree Garden Seeds

PO Box 300

New Gloucester, ME 04260

1-926-3400

http://www.superseeds.com/

The catalog claims over 900 varieties of seeds, bulbs, tubers, garden books and products. The listings are pretty extensive with the emphasis on vegetable seeds. There are sections for ethnic vegetables like Asian, Italian, and Latin American. The flower offerings include both annual and perennial flower seeds. The garden book section is impressive, boasting 14 pages of gardening related books. Several pages of garden supplies, there is

even a Garden-opoly game.

Seeds of Change

PO Box 15700

Santa Fe NM 87592-1500

1-888-762-7333

http://www.seedsofchange.com/

This catalog is for vegetable lovers as it is mostly devoted to them, and all seeds sold by this company are certified organic. There is a section of flower seeds, but veggies take center stage. There is a full

page of garlic varieties! Gourmet greens and herbs are in good supply, too.

There is also a good selection of gardening books and gardening supplies.

Select Seeds

180 Stickney Hill Road

Union, CT 06076

1-860-684-9310

http://www.selectseeds.com/

If you are looking for something a bit out of the mainstream or "different" then Select Seeds is the catalog you are looking for. Most of the seeds and plants offered are not found in the major outlets. Special sections for fragrant and old fashioned plants are featured. This catalog is a must for the home gardener looking for a flower garden that stands out a bit.

Seymours Selected Seeds

334 West Stroud Street

Randolph, WI 53596

1-800-353-9516

http://www.seymourseedusa.com/

This small catalog is packed with a full selection of annual and

perennial flowers for the home gardner. Many unusual varieties and

old time favorites. There is also a nice selection of bulbs and perennial

plants.

Southern Exposure Seed Exchange

PO Box 460

Mineral, VA 23117

Phone: 540-894-9480

Fax: 540-894-9481

http://www.southernexposure.com/

Annuals

Bulbs

Perennials

Exotic Plants and Flowers

Flower, Vegetable and Wildflower Seeds

Fruit Trees and Berries

Garden Supplies, Tools and Power Equipment

Gifts and Decorative Accessories

Ground Covers, Shrubs, Trees, and Vines

Herbs and Vegetables

Irrigation Supplies and Equipment

Fertilizer, Weed & Pest Control Products

Magazines and Books

Ornamental Grasses and Plants

Other

We are a wonderful source for vegetables selected in a day where taste and local adaptability were the primary factors. We have an extensive line of heirloom and other open pollinated seeds and seed saving supplies. Many of our varieties are certified organic. We also carry a wide variety of garlic and perennial onion bulbs and medicinal herb rootstock. We are a source for naturally colored cotton seeds. Many of our products are Certified Organic.

Website: www.southernexposure.com

Email Contact: gardens@southernexposure.com

Swallowtail Garden Seeds

122 Calistoga Road, #178

Santa Rosa, CA 95409

Phone: Toll Free 1-877-489-7333

707-538-3585

http://www.swallowtailgardenseeds.com/

Territorial Seed Company

PO Box 158

Cottate Grove, OR 97424

1-541-942-9547

http://www.territorialseed.com/

This is a good catalog for market gardeners. Territoral has a big selection of vegetables. There are a lot of different varieties of beans, with 25 pound bags available many varieties. Sweet and popcorn also well represented. Many varieties of lettuce also listed. Melons, peppers, peas, pumpkins and squash, along with boatloads of tomatoes. They also have a large selecion of annual flowers, available in larger quantities, so small greenhouse growers would find this catalog helpful. There are approximately 30 varieties of sunflowers, and lots of herbs. There is a good selection of growing supplies, including several types of spun bond fabric row covers. You will find a pretty good selection of organic growing aids in here also.Also a small selection of honey bee supplies, including a mason bee starter kit.

Thompson and Morgan

220 Faraday Ave

Jackson NJ 08527

1-800-274-7333

http://www.thompsonandmorgan.com/

200 pages of pure joy! Thompson and Morgan is one of the most complete seed catalogs available to the home gardener. You will find something of everything including the most popular annual and perennial flowers, vegetables and herbs, tree seeds and houseplants. There are hard to find varieties,

standard varieties and some downright odd and unusual varieties.

This catalog focuses on seeds, so you won't find many gardening supplies.

Thompson and Morgan is one seed catalog the serious gardener shouldn't be

without.

Totally Tomatoes

334 West Stroud Street

Randolph, WI 53956

1-800-345-5977

http://www.totallytomato.com/

41 pages of nothing but tomatoes. They have the standard varieties available everywhere like Burpee Big Boy and Park Whopper. But there are many hard to find varieties like Aunt Ruby's German Green, Dixie Golden Giant and Bloody Butcher. They also have a good selection of peppers (16 pages), salad greens and cucumbers. Nice catalog and very interesting.

Urban Farmer Seeds

4105 Indiana 32 West

Westfield, IN 46074

1-317-600-2807

customerservice@ufseeds.com

http://www.ufseeds.com/

Vermont Bean Seed Company

334 W Stroud Street

Randolph, WI 53956

800-349-1071

http://www.vermontbean.com/

These folks really do have the beans, sixteen pages of them. The catalog is chuck full of other stuff, too. Vegetable seeds are in good supply as well as some flower seeds and herbs. They also sell vegetable and flower plants.

Garden supplies include a nice selection of organic garden aids,and seed starting supplies.

Acknowledgements

https://en.wikipedia.org/wiki/Pea

http://www.garden.org/plantguide/?q=show&id=2118

https://www.libraries.psu.edu/psul/lifesciences/agnic/homegardening/vegindex/pea.html

http://www.onecommunityglobal.org/peas/

http://www.herbs2000.com/flowers/s_care.htm

http://eol.org/pages/703192/details

https://gobotany.newenglandwild.org/species/pisum/sativum/

http://www.the-compost-gardener.com/nitrogen-fixing-bacteria.html

http://www.the-compost-gardener.com/nitrogen-fixing-bacteria.html

http://www.nrcresearchpress.com/doi/abs/10.4141/cjps93-013

http://www.pickyourown.org/freezing_peas.htm

http://nchfp.uga.edu/how/can_04/peas_green_shelled.html

http://www.garden.org/plantguide/?q=show&id=2118

http://www.territorialseed.com/category/shelling_peas_seed

https://en.wikipedia.org/wiki/Pea

http://www.garden.org/plantguide/?q=show&id=2118

https://www.libraries.psu.edu/psul/lifesciences/agnic/homegardening/vegindex/pea.html

http://www.onecommunityglobal.org/peas/

http://www.herbs2000.com/flowers/s_care.htm

http://eol.org/pages/703192/details

https://gobotany.newenglandwild.org/species/pisum/sativum/

http://www.the-compost-gardener.com/nitrogen-fixing-bacteria.html

http://www.the-compost-gardener.com/nitrogen-fixing-bacteria.html

http://www.nrcresearchpress.com/doi/abs/10.4141/cjps93-013

http://www.pickyourown.org/freezing_peas.htm

http://nchfp.uga.edu/how/can_04/peas_green_shelled.html

About the Author

Gardening, history and travel seem an odd soup in which to stew one's life, but Paul has done just that. A gardener since 1975, he has spent his spare time reading history and traveling with his wife. He gardens, plans his travels and writes his books out in the sticks near a small town in southeast Indiana. He enjoys sharing the things he has learned about gardening, history and travel with his readers. The many books Paul has written reflect that joy of sharing. He also writes fiction in his spare time. Read and enjoy his books, if you will. Or dare.

Now, back to writing, if he can get the cat off the keyboard.

Join Paul on Facebook

https://www.facebook.com/Mossy-Feet-Books-474924602565571/

Twitter

https://twitter.com/MossyFeetBooks

mossyfeetbooks@gmail.com

Mossy Feet Books Catalog

To Get Your Free Copy of the Mossy Feet Books Catalogue, Click This Link.

http://mossyfeetbooks.blogspot.com/

Gardening Books

Fantasy Books

Humor

Science Fiction

Semi – Autobiographical Books

Travel Books

Back to Table of Contents

Sample – Gardener's Guide Garden Tools
Garden Trowels

A garden trowel is an indispensable tool for every gardener. All gardeners should have one trowel and it is best to have several for different purposes. The word trowel derives from the Latin word "truella", which means "small ladle". A trowel can serve as a ladle but that is really just one use for a trowel. Indeed, a trowel is the most used tool in the gardener's toolbox so it is important to get a good one. Nothing is as aggravating as a poor quality trowel that bends when you try to dig. Additionally, a poorly designed handle tires the hand and causes blisters.

There is an incredible variety of hand trowels available to the modern gardener. The gardener will find wood handle trowels and plastic composite trowels. Also available are aluminum and stainless steel trowels. New ergonomic designs make gardening easier on the hands. They also make it more accessible to those with repetitive stress injury and arthritis. These new designs include gel filled handles and curved designs that are more natural for the hand to hold while using them.

Finding a good garden hand trowel from this vast selection of trowels is a bit confusing. So take your time and then choose the garden hand trowel best suited for your needs.

Ergonomic Trowels

Ergonomic trowels use a new design to provide ergonomic ease of use. Some of the new ergonomic trowels help gardeners with arthritis continue their garden activities. These tools also help gardeners without those disorders to garden with less stress to their hands and wrists.

The ergonomic design of the trowel's handle allows the gardener to use a more natural position while working. A cushioned grip helps prevent blisters. These trowels are usually composed of an alloy consisting of cast aluminum and magnesium so they are light and strong. The blade's design allows you to punch into the soil easily and lift a manageable load of soil. The curved shapes provide a more balanced transfer of energy from the hand and wrist to the trowel. This reduces hand fatigue common when using a hand garden trowel.

Gel Ergonomic Trowels

Gel ergonomic trowels provide a cushioned grip that prevent blisters and make working in the garden more fun. Gardeners abuse their hands a lot with all that digging, pruning and chopping. Any tool which helps reduce that abuse is a welcome addition to any gardener's tool chest. A gel grip trowel helps your hands by incorporating a cushioned, gel filled handle into the garden trowel's design.

This gel flexes and provides cushioning to hard-working fingers while digging. Some of these feature a serrated edge to open bags of fertilizer or other gardening material and to cut roots while digging. Others have stainless steel blades.

Stainless Steel Trowels

Stainless steel is an ideal component to use to make trowels. It is strong, durable and resists rust. They also polish to a high sheen so they are attractive as well. The shiny metal is easy to spot if the gardener misplaced the tool while pursuing other projects in the garden. Stainless steel trowels usually have wood handles. These trowels are prone to rusting over time.

Nursery Trowels

The small, lightweight nursery trowel works well in tight spaces. The long handle of the nursery trowel allows you to reach into tight spots and the small, light blade makes it an ideal trowel for women to use.

Soil Scoop Trowels

A soil scoop is a specialized trowel that will certainly find many uses in and around the garden. The scoop is great for those who mix their own potting soil, as it will allow you to scoop vermiculate, peat moss and other soil components. The scoop will also work great to pot up plants and fill bedding packs for small transplants. Using the scoop, you can pick up potting soil from the bag or bin and place it where you want it. This help to fill in around roots under and around stems and leaves.

A soil scoop will work better than a trowel to fill in soil around newly transplanted shrubs and flowers in the garden. It can also scoop fertilizer and other bulk garden products into spreaders. Specialized bonsai soil scoops work great to fill soil in and around the small pots used in bonsai. Their unique shape fits in under the leaves and branches of these miniature trees better than a trowel. The right soil scoop fills a void left by the hand trowel. Standard trowels are great for digging and weeding. However, their shape is usually not suitable for scooping soil for potting and bonsai needs.

Aluminum Trowel

Aluminum trowels are strong, durable and lightweight. Aluminum resists corrosion, so if you accidentally leave your trowel out in the rain it will not rust. Since aluminum trowels are cast in one piece, the blade will not separate from the handle, as it will with some other types of trowels. Aluminum is a soft metal and it will not hold a sharp edge as a steel trowel will. Since it is not a strong as steel, aluminum garden trowels may bend easier if you are digging in heavy soil. The blades of an aluminum trowel may also chip if you strike a rock while digging. Aluminum trowels usually have a plastic grip on the handle to cushion your hand. Rubberized grips are easier on the hand than the polypropylene ones.

Wood Handle Trowels

The traditional handle for a garden trowel has been wood. Wood, usually a hardwood like ash or hickory, is the traditional choice for a handle for a trowel. Attractive, strong and durable many manufacturers still make trowels with wood handles. However, it tends to split, especially if you accidentally leave the trowel out in the weather.

Trowel Maintenance

Protect the trowel from rust with a coating of old motor oil or cooking oil when not in use. A good spray with aerosol cooking oil before using will make the trowel easier to clean when finished with it. Alternatively, fill a bucket with sand and saturate it with oil. Use this to dip your hand tools in to clean them and add a protective sheen of oil to help prevent rust. Sometimes it is helpful to file or grind the edges of steel trowels to a sharp edge to make it easier to cut into soil. Paint the handles or blades a bright orange or yellow to make them more visible. This makes it less likely to lose the trowel or leave it out in the weather.

The wide variety of trowels on the market can intimidate even the most seasoned gardener. Trowels come in different shapes, sizes, materials and colors. Picking the right type of trowel is easier if the gardener is aware of the many different types available and the uses of each.

Mossy Feet Books
www.mossyfeetbooks.com

Printed in Great Britain
by Amazon